MONSTER TRUCKS
THE NEED FOR SPEED

Mike Johnstone

LERNER
SPORTS
AN IMPRINT OF LERNER PUBLISHING GROUP

CREDITS

First American edition published in 2002 by LernerSports

Original edition published in 2001 by Franklin Watts

This book is available in two editions:
Library binding by LernerSports
Soft cover by First Avenue Editions
Imprints of Lerner Publishing Group
241 First Avenue North
Minneapolis, MN 55401 U.S.A.
Website address: www.lernerbooks.com

Picture credits: *Front cover: Allsport UK Ltd, (middle and bottom Tim DeFrisco) Back cover: Allsport UK Ltd, pp. 1 main and inset, Andrew Fielder, 2-3 left Andrew Fielder, middle Eric Stern, right Andrew Fielder, 4-5 main and inset Andrew Fielder, 6-7 main Allsport UK Ltd (Ron Hornaday) inset Allsport UK Ltd (Kevin Cywinski), 8-9 main (Mike Wallace), inset (Kevin Harvick), 10-11 Andrew Fielder, 12-13 Andrew Fielder, 14-15 Andrew Fielder, 16-17 Andrew Fielder, 18-19 Eric Stern, 20-21 Eric Stern, 22-23 Andrew Fielder, 24-25 Andrew Fielder, 26-27 Eric Stern, 30-31 left and middle Andrew Fielder, inset Allsport UK Ltd (Kevin Cywinski)*

Library of Congress Cataloging-in-Publication Data

Johnstone, Michael, 1946-
  Monster trucks / by Michael Johnstone.
      p. cm. — (The need for speed)
Includes index.
Summary: Describes and illustrates various forms of truck racing and related events, including NASCAR truck racing, monster truck racing, and car crushing events.
  ISBN 0-8225-0388-3 (lib. bdg.)
  ISBN 0-8225-0391-3 (pbk.)
  1. Truck racing—Juvenile literature. 2. Monster trucks— Juvenile literature. [1. Truck racing. 2. Monster trucks. 3. Trucks.] I. Title. II. Series.
  GV1034.996 .J62 2002
  796.7—dc21   *2001003360*

Bound in the United States of America
1 2 3 4 5 6 – OS – 07 06 05 04 03 02

CONTENTS

INTRODUCTION

If you've ever seen truck or monster-truck racing live or on television, you may have wondered what it's like to sit in the cockpit of one of these amazing machines.

The Need for Speed puts you in the driver's seat of some of the most famous trucks in the game as they roar around a racetrack or thunder toward empty cars, about to turn them into piles of tangled and twisted metal.

The trucks featured in this book include the granddaddy of them all—Bigfoot, which became the first monster car crusher less than 25 years ago. Since then, the popularity of truck racing and monster-truck racing has taken off.

The vehicles may have different names, but all monster trucks have features in common. These include huge engines, enormous tires, and the need for speed.

As well as giving you a taste of the thrills of truck racing and monster-truck racing, we'll also provide some facts and figures behind these incredible machines. These are found in the Stat Files and Fact Files, which look like this:

STAT FILE

Black Stallion

Make	Ford F-150
Weight	10,028 lbs (4,549 kg)
Height	10 ft (3 m)

4

NASCAR and ARCA Truck Racing

Recognizing the growing interest in truck racing, NASCAR (National Association for Stock Car Auto Racing) first organized a few exhibition races in 1994. The response from fans was so positive that NASCAR sanctioned an entire season the following year. In 1998 ARCA (Automobile Racing Club of America) also decided to organize a couple of exhibition truck races, and the following year it added a full season of truck racing.

Fact Files give you slightly unusual, strange, or funny information.

FACT FILE

Pricey Power

Rules limit monster-truck engines to 575 cubic inches (9,423 cubic centimeters). Custom-built for extra power, a decent engine makes a hole of around $28,000 in a monster trucker's bank account!

NASCAR CRAFTSMAN TRUCKS

When NASCAR officials started to research the potential of truck racing as a spectator sport, the strength of the response surprised them.

It wasn't long before a sponsor—Craftsman Tools—came forward to put money into the sport. This allowed for the creation of a new series of vehicles on the race circuit—NASCAR Craftsman trucks.

The trucks are built in modular style (with separate, easily replaceable body parts). They are rear-wheel driven and built to withstand rough, tough driving. But perhaps the trucks' main attraction for the people who race them is that the drivers can do much of the maintenance themselves.

NASCAR rules stipulate that the trucks' engines must run on a 9:1 compression ratio, which limits the speed they can reach.

FACT FILE

The main difference between driving a Craftsman truck and a NASCAR stock car is the truck's increased wheelbase. The bigger size affects chassis loading and weight distribution, making the trucks a challenge to handle.

NASCAR CRAFTSMAN TRUCKS

With safety as their top priority, many experts want NASCAR's 9:1 compression rule to be applied across the stock-racing board. The research put into developing Craftsman trucks will be vital in deciding whether this happens.

An exciting sport in its own right, Craftsman truck racing is also an excellent training ground for the NASCAR stock-car drivers of tomorrow.

A beginner who can put a truck through its paces in a NASCAR truck race develops the skills that will enable him (or, increasingly, her) to take to the wheel of a stock car and power it around Daytona, Indianapolis, or any of the tracks on the NASCAR circuit.

Dubbed "supertruck racing," the sport gives aspiring stock-car drivers great experience.

FACT FILE

On to a Winner

NASCAR's decision to back truck racing has paid off, not just in terms of increasing attendance at racetracks, but because of the opportunities it gives for research and development. For example, truck drivers help try out new kinds of engines.

THE BIG BOYS

In addition to NASCAR Craftsman truck racing and ARCA truck racing, there's monster-truck racing—a sport that has thrilled thousands coast to coast for more than 25 years. The sport is spreading to Britain, Sweden, and other European countries.

It all started in the mid-1970s, when a number of pick-up fans started to experiment with making their trucks bigger and better. One of the first to do so was Bob Chandler, who owned a business specializing in selling four-wheel-drive vehicles. Between 1976 and 1982, Bob added bigger and bigger tires to his Ford F-250 pickup, improved its suspension, and put in rear steering.

In 1981, as a way of publicizing his business, Chandler bought a couple of old wrecks from a local junkyard close to St. Louis, Missouri, and drove them to a nearby cornfield. He set up a video camera, revved the engine of his hybrid pickup, and sent it roaring toward the old jalopies. A few seconds later, they were little more than a pile of compressed metal!

Bob put the video on a loop in his showroom. His customers loved it. A few months later, in April 1982, an enterprising promoter convinced Chandler to repeat the crush, this time in front of an audience. The crush took place in Jefferson, Missouri. Several thousand people paid to watch it, and a new sport was born—monster trucking.

Truck fests are held around the United States and, increasingly, in other countries. The regular appearances of monster trucks on television, especially satellite and cable television, is making monster-truck racing a popular sport all over the world.

Pricey Power

Rules limit monster-truck engines to 575 cubic inches (9,423 cubic centimeters). Custom-built for extra power, a decent engine makes a hole of around $28,000 in a monster trucker's bank account!

SPEED . . .
AND SAFETY

Monster trucks are built for high-power bursts of speed. They generate between 1,500 and 2,000 horsepower and reach speeds of up to 100 miles per hour (160 kilometers per hour).

In car-jump events, they can fly through the air as far as 115 feet (35 meters) and sometimes gain a height of 25 ft (7.5 m).

Safety rules demand that each truck be fitted with three ignition interruptor switches. The switches are checked each time a truck comes up to the starting line, no matter how often that occurs at any one event.

Drivers wear a five-point safety harness, a neck collar, gloves, and a fireproof suit.

The number of cars a monster truck has to jump in competition varies from stadium to stadium and depends on the length of the track. In general, at indoor shows, drivers attempt to get their trucks over 18 cars and, at outdoor events, over as many as 25 cars side to side. As with crush events, cars are usually bought from local junkyards.

Most monster trucks have continuous fiberglass bodies with no door. The driver and any passengers climb into the cab through a manhole on the passenger-side floorboard.

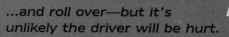

After a jump, a truck can land with a bang...

...and roll over—but it's unlikely the driver will be hurt.

Staying Safe

Under competition rules, all monster trucks have to be fitted with a minimum eight-point, steel roll cage. They must also have an approved fire extinguisher system that the driver can operate with his or her eyes closed from the seat-belted position. In every vehicle, a firewall protects the driver's compartment against an engine fire. Rules also specify that the windshield should be made of a shatterproof material called Lexan.

WHAT A CRUSH!

Most monster-truck events feature a mixture of races, jumps, and freestyle stunts, but it's the car crushes that bring the audiences to their feet.

Monster-truck drivers zip themselves into their suits, clamber onto the tires, and pull themselves up into their cabins. When the engines leap to life and the drivers put their 4-x-4 monsters into gear, the trucks start to vibrate violently. As they roar around the arena, the drivers perform wheelies and other tricks that show off their skills.

Then the trucks get into position and wait for the green starting light. The first driver to go pulls the restraining straps as tightly as possible and puts a foot down hard on the accelerator. The thrust generated by the massive engine pushes the driver back into the seat as the truck races toward the line of parked cars.

When impact occurs, the cars that were once in the driver's sights vanish from view as the truck's front tires crunch into them. Using all of his (or her) expertise, the driver raises the truck onto its back wheels, like some prehistoric monster rearing up to devour its prey.

Seconds after the rear tires crunch into the cars, the driver brings the truck crashing down, then races away. What a few moments before was a line of scrapped but still recognizable cars has become a sad pile of twisted metal. Roofs have been slammed into floors, bumpers are sticking out at weird angles, and fragments of ripped upholstery flap in the breeze. Then the rest of the drivers take their turns.

The crush over, it's time for the audience to make its way home and for the drivers to wind down, check their trucks for any damage, and get ready for the next event—which may be hundreds of miles away.

FACT FILE

An Expensive Game

Running a monster truck costs money—big money. The vehicles have to be hauled from stadium to stadium and maintained in excellent condition. All this can cost more than $100,000 a year.

For weeks before a truck event, organizers scour junkyards for old cars to crush.

15

BIGFOOT

In 1983 Bob Chandler's company arranged a sponsorship deal with Ford. Since then a total of 16 of his Bigfoot monster trucks have thrilled U.S. spectators coast to coast and television audiences around the world.

It's not just Bigfoot that has benefited from the deal. Since 1983 the Ford F series, on which Bigfoot is based, has become the world's best-selling truck, partly because of the popularity of monster-truck racing.

Bigfoot became such a success that by 1985 more and more enthusiasts were starting to adapt their own trucks, making monsters out of production-line models. Car crushes began to draw bigger and bigger crowds.

Within a year or two, however, spectators wanted something new, so monster-truck owners started to race their amazing creations against one another and to make their trucks sail over jumps.

This new phase of the sport quickly caught on, both at live events and when satellite and cable television companies began to air the sport.

Versatile Bigfoot is a favorite at crush events...

...and also at jumps and races all over the United States.

BEARFOOT CHEVROLET

Built in 1979, Bearfoot was one of the first monster trucks to take to the sporting scene.

Fred Shafer, Bearfoot's creator, remained one of the biggest names in the sport until his retirement in 1998. For 18 years, Fred and his wife Kathy traveled all over the United States, entertaining audiences at major events and smaller state fairs.

Shafer began his racing career on the Drag Racing circuit in 1965 when he was 18 years old. He quickly established himself as one of the most competent drivers. By the end of the 1970s, he was eager to try his hand at something new. He and a friend, Jack WIllman, bought a 1979 Chevrolet pickup truck, beefed up the frame, and replaced the standard Chevrolet axles with five-ton military ones. They also fitted the truck with monster-sized 66-in (1.66-m) Goodyear tires.

Weighing over eight tons, the truck was so successful that within 10 years seven more monster trucks had been added to the Bearfoot fleet.

STAT FILE

Bearfoot Chevrolet

Make	Chevrolet
Weight	8 tons/7.3 tonnes
Tires	66-in (1.6-m) Goodyear
Engine	454 ci (7,439 cc)
Suspension	Heavy-duty leaf springs

By 1991 Fred Shafer had built the Chevrolet-based Bearfoot team into one of the leaders in the world of monster trucks. He realized that, for his team to stay at the top, he needed more funds to finance future expansion.

After several months of secret negotiations, the team announced that Bearfoot was abandoning Chevrolet in favor of Dodge.

The first fruit of the Dodge/Shafer collaboration was Bearfoot 10, a fiberglass-bodied monster based on the Dodge Dakota pickup. It became an immediate hit with Dodge dealers (who vied with each other to book the vehicle in their areas to promote their trucks). It found success on the racetrack, too. In 1992 the vehicle won the Camel World Championship. As with his Chevrolet-based Bearfoot, Shafer had a nail-biting wait—until the last race of the season—to find out that he had won the title.

The following year saw the introduction of Bearfoot 11, again based on the Dodge Dakota. The 572 ci (9373 cc) dry-block engine (one that has no coolant water in it) gave 1500 hp and was positioned below the driver, about 3 ft (0.9 m) off the ground—a new twist that initially caused many problems.

Dodge got its money's worth out of its sponsorship deal with Bearfoot. Fred Shafer's team clinched not only the World Championship title but several world speed records as well.

STAT FILE

Bearfoot Dodge

Make	Dodge Dakota
Engine	572 ci (9,373 cc) dry-block, 1500 hp

FACT FILE

TV Stars

Two trucks from Fred Shafer's stable were featured in the 1980s TV series Knight Rider. They collided and appeared to burst into flames, courtesy of the TV studio's special effects department.

BLACK STALLION 2000

Maryland monster trucker Mike Vaters drove into the new millennium in an updated version of his highly rated Black Stallion, called Black Stallion 2000.

Built around a 2000 Ford F-150 pickup, Black Stallion 2000 has four-link suspension with custom-built sway bars, Rockwell 106 axles, and 66-in (1.6-m) tires.

From cabin top to tire bottom, Black Stallion 2000 stands 11 ft (3.4 m) high and is 12 feet (3.6 m) wide.

Some drivers can leap their trucks over two dozen cars in one stride. At a four-wheel-drive event in Philadelphia, Mike Vaters went one better. He jumped over another monster truck—Andy Hoffman's Nitemare!

To pull off a trick like that and come down to earth without too much of a bang, a truck needs an awesome suspension. Black Stallion 2000 gets it from a KS Nitro Shock Suspension system—the best in the business. The shocks are fully adjustable to vehicle weight and ride height. They work in each direction of travel through hydraulic valving and need no other mechanical springs.

At almost 5 tons, Black Stallion is a real crusher!

In a thrilling moment, Black Stallion flies over Nitemare.

Black Stallion

Make	Ford F-150
Weight	10,028 lbs (4,549 kg)
Height	11 ft (3 m)

EXECUTIONER

Based in Illinois and owned and driven by brothers Tim and Mark Hall, Executioner is a great crowd pleaser at monster-truck events.

Tim Hall, one of monster-truck racing's most influential players, became president of the Monster Truck Racing Association in 1997. Executioner was one of the top five trucks in both the 1996 PENDA points series and the following year's Special Events points series. It was named truck of the year in 1996, the same year that the Halls were awarded most improved team of the year and that Mark Hall was named driver of the year.

Executioner is a 1999 Dodge Ram pickup, powered by a 515 ci (8439 cc) supercharged, alcohol-burning engine that delivers 1000 hp. The Lenco air-shift transmission permits smooth gear changing. The eight KS nitrogen shock absorbers and the 4–link suspension give the driver a smooth ride. The Hall brothers built the tubular racing chassis themselves. Executioner's massive Goodyear Terra tires are more than 1.5 ft (0.5 m) deep.

EXECUTIONER

Expensive Monster
Like all vehicles registered with
the Monster Truck Racing
Association, Executioner has a
certified value for insurance
purposes—$110,000.

STAT FILE

Executioner	
Make	Dodge Ram
Engine	515 ci (8,439 cc) alcohol-burning

KING KRUNCH

When it comes to crunching cars, King Krunch lives up to its name, as the 60,000 fans who crammed into the Houston Astrodome in January 2000 can testify. That was the night when 16 of the top names in monster trucking thundered onto the field to battle each other. At the end of the night, King Krunch reigned supreme.

The truck is owned and driven by Scott Stephens from Spring, Texas. Scott has been driving monster trucks since 1980. He was among the first drivers to experiment with turbine-powered aircraft engines in monster trucks. This kind of engine makes flames shoot out from under the hood, delighting spectators.

King Krunch is based on a 1999 Dodge Ram pickup and is powered by a 572 ci (9373 cc) engine. It is proving to be very successful. In addition to the truck's triumph in Houston, it placed third at the Pace Motor Sports Monster Trucking World Finals in Las Vegas.

In 2000 King Krunch regularly featured among the top 10 competing trucks of the United States Hot Rod Association (USHRA) monster-truck circuit.

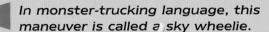
In monster-trucking language, this maneuver is called a sky wheelie.

STAT FILE

King Krunch

Make	1999 Dodge Ram
Engine	572 ci (9,373 cc)

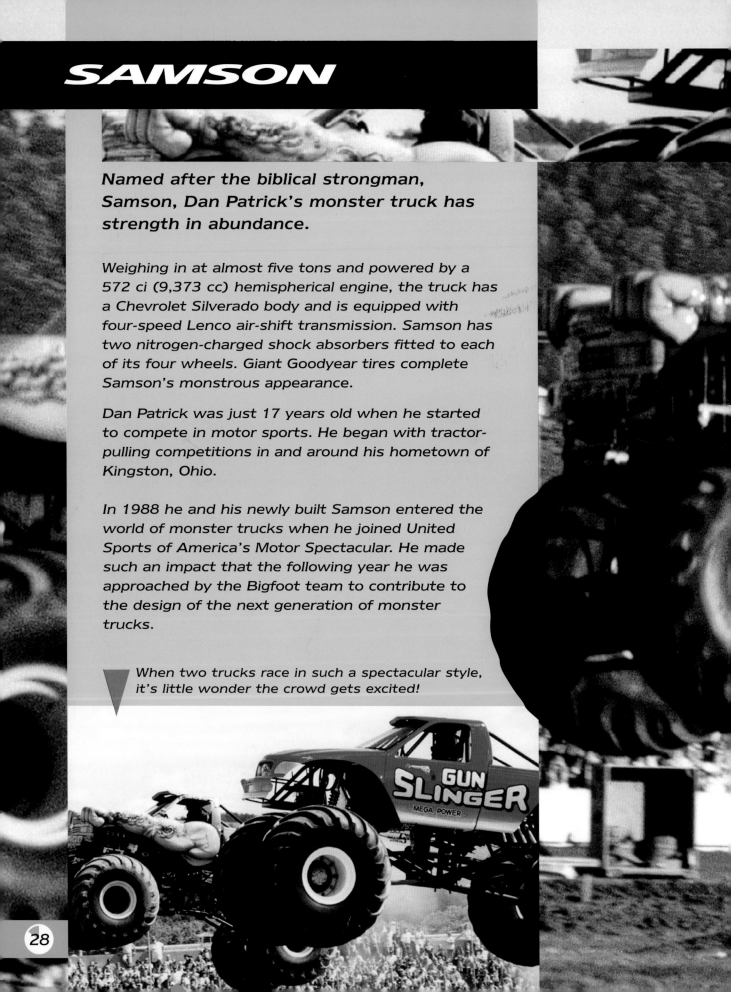

SAMSON

Named after the biblical strongman, Samson, Dan Patrick's monster truck has strength in abundance.

Weighing in at almost five tons and powered by a 572 ci (9,373 cc) hemispherical engine, the truck has a Chevrolet Silverado body and is equipped with four-speed Lenco air-shift transmission. Samson has two nitrogen-charged shock absorbers fitted to each of its four wheels. Giant Goodyear tires complete Samson's monstrous appearance.

Dan Patrick was just 17 years old when he started to compete in motor sports. He began with tractor-pulling competitions in and around his hometown of Kingston, Ohio.

In 1988 he and his newly built Samson entered the world of monster trucks when he joined United Sports of America's Motor Spectacular. He made such an impact that the following year he was approached by the Bigfoot team to contribute to the design of the next generation of monster trucks.

▼ When two trucks race in such a spectacular style, it's little wonder the crowd gets excited!

FACT FILE

Moving the Monster

Samson is featured at more than 100 truck events a year. The truck is transported from show to show on a custom-built transporter that comes equipped with living quarters and a repair shop.

USEFUL CONTACTS

If you are interested in truck or monster-truck racing, here are some names and numbers that might be useful.

Automobile Racing Club of America
P.O. Box 5217
Toledo, Ohio 43611

NASCAR
P.O. Box 2875
Daytona Beach, Florida 32120
email: publicrelations@nascar.com
www.nascar.com

Professional Racing Organization
P.O. Box 4327
Portsmouth, New Hampshire 03802

Rally Race Trucks
P.O. Box 1136
Coshocton, Ohio 43812

Short Track Super Trucks
P.O. Box 3227
Chilton, Wisconsin 53014

WEBSITES

Andrew Fielder's Monster Trucks
www.monstertrucks-uk.com

Bigfoot 4 x 4
www.bigfoot4x4.com

Fourwheeler Magazine Online
www.fourwheeler.com

Eric Stern
www.monstertruckracing.com

Gun Slinger Monster Truck
www.gunslinger4x4.com

Jurassic Attack Monster Truck
www.jurassicattack.com

Mike's Monster Trucks
www.mikesmonstertrucks.com

Sudden Impact Monster Truck
www.suddenimpact.com

Special Events: The Promotion Company
www.familyevents.com

Truckworld
www.truckworld.com

U.S. Hot Rod Association
www.ushra.com

A LANGUAGE OF ITS OWN

bite: traction

burn out/dry hop: to clear the truck's tires of mud by spinning them

cut tires: to shave the tread off the tires to gain bite or lose weight

donut: to spin circles in one spot in the arena

eyeball the track: to survey the track or competition

good hookin' clay: track dirt that makes it easy for the tires to hook up

grab a footful: to jump on the accelerator

grenade: to badly damage an engine or other truck part

hole shot: first vehicle off the starting line

hook up: to take off fast from the starting line by digging in the tires

hot shoe: a top driver

lose fire: to stall the engine

pogo: an action that results when a truck comes down hard and causes the rear end to bounce up and down repeatedly

power out: to use a burst of acceleration to keep the truck from rolling

pull the pin: to remove the emergency pin in the rear bumper to shut off the power

red light: to leave the starting line early, before the green starting light signals

sky wheelie: a move that occurs when a truck's front end drops onto an object and causes the rear end to stand straight up

teeter: to wheelie the front end with the rear tires on the ground and cause the truck to rock from side to side

tranny: the transmission that transfers power from the engine to the drive train

wheelie: to get the truck up on its rear wheels, lifting the front off the ground

INDEX